THEN & NOW

FORT MYERS

Opposite: Thomas A. Edison, with Mina Edison at his side, unties the ribbon to open the mile-long, modern concrete Edison Bridge at the foot of Fowler Street. The inventor made a special trip to dedicate the bridge on his 84th birthday, February 11, 1931, only a few months before his death. The dedication had worldwide news coverage and was attended by numerous celebrities. Ironically, the bridge named for the inventor of the lightbulb was not lit until late 1937. (Then, courtesy Southwest Florida Historical Society.)

THEN & NOW

FORT MYERS

Gerri Reaves

To all who shared their memories of Fort Myers

Copyright © 2007 by Gerri Reaves
ISBN 978-0-7385-5354-2

Library of Congress control number: 2007938168

Published by Arcadia Publishing
Charleston SC, Chicago IL, Portsmouth NH, San Francisco CA

Printed in the United States of America

For all general information contact Arcadia Publishing at:
Telephone 843-853-2070
Fax 843-853-0044
E-mail sales@arcadiapublishing.com
For customer service and orders:
Toll-Free 1-888-313-2665

Visit us on the Internet at www.arcadiapublishing.com

ON THE FRONT COVER: The three-story Kress Building opened on December 1, 1927. John Morgan Dean teamed up with Lucius Currian Curtright and Frank C. Alderman to build it on the southwest corner of First Street and Broadway. Kress leased the building for 50 years. Today this showpiece of downtown redevelopment houses Starbucks and other businesses. (Then, courtesy Southwest Florida Museum of History; Now, courtesy the author.)

ON THE BACK COVER: This westward view of First Street is framed by the seven-story Franklin Arms Hotel, Fort Myers's first skyscraper (left), and the Work Projects Administration–constructed post office. Walter P. Franklin opened the eight-story hotel addition in 1924, having built onto Hill House, which was established in 1889 by Mary F. Hill. The post office is now the Sidney and Berne Davis Art Center. (Then, courtesy Southwest Florida Historical Society.)

CONTENTS

ACKNOWLEDGMENTS

Many people have graciously shared their personal knowledge about Fort Myers and helped me to envision its past alongside its present. I particularly thank Sara Nell Gran for her contributions to my research because without her many of my questions would have remained unanswered. Victor Zarick of the Southwest Florida Museum of History deserves special thanks; his expertise and humor were essential for this project. Always helpful and generous with their time at the Southwest Florida Historical Society were Helen Farrell, Doug Bartleson, Pete and Genevieve Bowen, and Dickie and Pat Jungferman.

I am grateful to historian Kathryn Wilbur for generously sharing her research and for our lively and encouraging talks about all things historical. Frank Pavese never failed to answer my questions, and Thomas Goolsby Stewart, Ph.D., and Carolyn Webber kindly contributed the vintage photograph of Stewart's Drug Store.

Taking the "now" photographs proved to be a challenging and fascinating task for me. I thank all the kind souls who moved a parked automobile, held a tree limb out of the picture frame, moved signs, led a kayak adventure, held a ladder, or just pointed me in the right direction: Suzanne Sutton and Jerry Haberle; Trey Raulerson; Connie Langmann, GAEA Guides; Jeremy Primus and Jeremy Comer, City of Fort Myers; John Yarbrough, director, Lee County Parks and Recreation; and Michela Meucci, Cella Molnar and Associates. Others who deserve recognition are general manager Matt Johnson and the staff at the Southwest Florida Museum of History, Sahid Kazemi of the engineering department of the City of Fort Myers, Booch DeMarchi of Lee County Public Resources, and the Lee County Black Historical Society. I took all of the modern photographs.

I acknowledge my indebtedness to Florida's superb state archives, the *Fort Myers News-Press* archives, and the writers whose historical work I merely add to: Karl H. Grismer, Prudy Taylor Board, Esther B. Colcord, Marian Bailey Godown, Alberta Colcord Barnes, Gregg Turner, Stan Mulford, Tom Smoot, Nell Colcord Weidenbach, and Patricia Pope Bartlett.

A heartfelt thank-you goes to Ken Rasi, Isabel Thies, and Lorin Arundel of the *River Weekly News* for the space and encouragement to pursue my passion for history.

For his expert eye, photography tutorials, and endless patience, I thank my husband and best friend, Jim Brock.

INTRODUCTION

Fort Myers's current wave of downtown redevelopment has put the spotlight on the public riverfront spaces and the city's history. Like other communities across the nation, Fort Myers strives to strike a balance between private and public needs, between historic preservation and development. The recent rechristening of downtown as the River District fittingly and symbolically links the city's newly emerging identity to its historic one. In 1990, the commercial district was added to the National Register of Historic Places. In 2003, the city adopted a master plan by renowned city planner Andres Duany. Ironically, that New Urbanist plan in many ways fulfills the 1926 Swan plan that was not fully implemented because of the 1920s economic bust.

These then and now images document the city's evolution from river wilderness to a 21st-century city once again reinventing itself. Long-gone is the wilderness by the river, the U.S. Army fort founded in the Seminole Indian Wars, and the cow town born in the March 1886 incorporation. But the physical traces of the town built by pioneers, poor or wealthy, full-time resident or snowbird, scrub farmer, merchant, or entrepreneur—those traces remain. Late-19th- and early-20th-century structures still mark the blocks where optimism, hard work, and ingenuity triumphed. The spirits, the voices, and the lives of generations are written in the very buildings and the visible layers of change. Trails and shell-rock paths lie beneath the roads and sidewalks of today. The river, the docks, the skyline—even the old oak trees—whisper of slower times when the arrival of the mail boat or the passenger train punctuated daily life in the "City of Palms."

This river town with its uncommon subtropical beauty has been discovered many times—by pioneers, Northern investors, tourists who launched the tarpon-fishing craze, post–World War II soldiers who decided to settle here and precipitated an economic boom, and so many others. Each discoverer experienced a private enchantment, a private dream. City plans, generations, booms and busts, war and peace have all come and gone. But there will always be the Caloosahatchee River and the sky. Seawalls and in-fill development have changed the location of the riverbank more than once, but the wide river is still the heart of Fort Myers, the reason for Fort Myers, and her people will always gather by it to work and celebrate.

FIRST THERE WAS A RIVER

The 1914 view of the Hendry (left) and Jackson Street docks pinpoints the birthplace of Fort Myers. After Fort Myers's 1885 incorporation, the town built a wharf at the foot of Jackson Street paralleling the Hendry Street dock first built in 1852. In the foreground is the staff headquarters of the U.S. Army post dating from the Seminole Indian Wars. (Then, courtesy Southwest Florida Historical Society.)

The 1889 photograph shows the "end of the road" for First Street where it seems to drop off into the river just west of Monroe Street. Starting in the 1920s, in-fill development extended the riverfront significantly. Today condominium towers rise from what once was the Caloosahatchee riverbed on the north side of West First Street. Until the 1960s, railroad tracks ran down the center of Monroe Street to the river. (Then, courtesy Southwest Florida Museum of History.)

FIRST THERE WAS A RIVER

Winter Home Thos. A. Edison, Fort Myers, Fla.

In 1885, Thomas A. Edison sailed up the Caloosahatchee River from Punta Rassa in search of bamboo to use as filament in his new invention, the lightbulb. He landed in the hamlet of Fort Myers and within hours bought 13 acres of riverfront property just south of downtown. Since 1909, the land around Seminole Lodge has been transformed from Florida wilderness to living laboratory to a cultivated estate on the National Register of Historic Places. (Then, courtesy State Archives of Florida.)

Once the world's largest citrus packing plant, the Lee County Packing Company opened in 1910 at the foot of Monroe Street and extended across the Caloosahatchee River. The Atlantic Coastline Railroad shipped hundreds of thousands of crates of fruit and produce in ventilated cars to a nation hungry for Florida's products. The plant burned in January 1914, was rebuilt, and burned again in the 1950s. Today's Fort Myers, as seen from Centennial Park, lacks the industrial flavor of decades ago. (Then, courtesy Southwest Florida Historical Society.)

The completion of the Fremont Bridge in 1924 in East Fort Myers helped precipitate the Fort Myers land and building boom of the 1920s. Seen below in 1925, the 16-foot-wide wooden bridge spanned the Caloosahatchee River and connected Fort Myers with North Fort Myers. As a segment of the Tamiami Trail, it later linked Tampa and Miami. The bridge was upstaged by the modern Edison Bridge in 1931 and was destroyed by fire in the 1940s. (Then, courtesy Southwest Florida Historical Society.)

At the old city dock at the foot of Jackson Street customers could venture right onto the wooden planks in Ford Model Ts to catch the Kinzie Brothers' steamboat or patronize the City Fish Market, the Chinese laundry, Raymond's Machine Shop, the Mogar Cigar Factory, or taxidermist Ike Shaw. In the post-1911 photograph below, Bay Street marks the river's edge. Today Jackson Street extends two full blocks from where it once joined the dock. (Then, courtesy Southwest Florida Historical Society.)

FIRST THERE WAS A RIVER

In 1927, the City of Fort Myers completed a recreation pier, a Moorish-style auditorium called the Pleasure Palace, and a municipal pool at the foot of Heitman Street. The pier (right) ran underneath today's Caloosahatchee River Bridge. Pictured above in the early 1940s, the pier was demolished in 1943, and the auditorium was moved to Edwards Drive and renamed the Hall of Fifty States. The pool was destroyed in the 1960s when the bridge was built. (Then, courtesy Southwest Florida Historical Society.)

In the 1930 photograph, Frank Pellegrin, owner of the Gondola Inn, stands in front of his just-opened seafood restaurant that actually floated on the Caloosahatchee River west of Carson Street. The Pleasure Pier is shown in the right background. Eventually the restaurant was raised onto dock pilings. The popular Joe's Crab Shack now occupies this prime spot where mangroves grow under the steps at the river's edge and generations have enjoyed a classic view and a meal. (Then, courtesy Southwest Florida Museum of History.)

FIRST THERE WAS A RIVER

CHAPTER 2

HOMES AND HOTELS

In 1897, Hugh O'Neill, a wealthy New York City merchant, bought the Hendry House, razed it, and built a state-of-the-art riverfront hotel at the foot of Royal Palm Avenue. In 1898, the Royal Palm Hotel's much-publicized opening launched Fort Myers's tourism industry. Visible on the horizon in 1927 is the Seaboard Air Line Railway bridge. The Gilded Age hotel survived until 1948. (Then, courtesy Southwest Florida Historical Society.)

The Hendry House on the Caloosahatchee River was the homestead of Capt. Francis Asbury and Ardeline Lanier Hendry, one of Fort Myers's founding families. In 1889, their son Louis A. Hendry bought the family home, added 14 rooms, and converted the house into the Hendry House Hotel. Long a convenience for steamboat passengers in that pre-railroad era, the hotel was demolished in 1897. Now the Ramada Inn accommodates travelers eager to discover Fort Myers. (Then, courtesy State Archives of Florida.)

The Riverview Hotel, originally the Keystone, sheltered Thomas Edison during his first visit to the area in 1885. When Edison returned in March 1886 with his bride, Mina, they resided at the Keystone until their new home was ready for occupancy. The Riverside is pictured above at its post-1895 location on First Street, *c.* 1921. Amenities included hot and cold sulphur baths and 640 feet of porch. No longer riverside, this site is a city garage with storefronts. (Then, courtesy Southwest Florida Historical Society.)

The Vivas home on First Street was on the homestead purchased by Joseph Delores and Christiana Stirrup Vivas (left), who arrived in Fort Myers in March 1866 as honeymooners. They lived in a log cabin between Lee Street and Royal Palm Avenue until 1883, when they constructed this house on the same site. In 1925, the home site with 132 feet of frontage sold for $250,000. Today's First Street Center is being developed where two of the city's first pioneers settled. (Then, courtesy Southwest Florida Historical Society.)

The Hotel Seminole (below) hosts a group of Iowans in 1916. The wood-frame building with a wide wraparound porch and rocking chairs typifies the style of buildings and homes that all but disappeared from downtown during the 1920s building boom. Located on Lee Street between First and Second Streets, the boarding hotel was named the Everglades Hotel around the turn of the 20th century but had expanded and changed its name by 1914. Today the hotel site is the Embarq parking lot. (Then, courtesy Southwest Florida Historical Society.)

Montana cattleman John T. Murphy built this three-story Colonial Revival–style home in 1901 at First and Fowler Streets on the riverfront. In 1918, Thomas and Adeline Hill Phipps Burroughs acquired the house, which features a wraparound verandah and a widow's walk. Their daughter Mona Burroughs Fischer bequeathed the house to the city in 1978. Pictured below in 1929, the home is now listed in the National Register of Historic Places. Many of the furnishings and heirlooms are original to the Burroughs family. (Then, courtesy Southwest Florida Museum of History.)

The 1925 Alderman-Paul House is one of Fort Myers's most picturesque Spanish Revival–style residences of the real estate–boom era. It features a central front arcade with blue and gold Italian tiles, wrought-iron balconies, spiral columns, barrel-roof tiles, and ornate medallions. Facing the Caloosahatchee River on First Street, it was one of many homes along Millionaires Row. Listed on the National Register of Historic Places in 1988, today it is the office of the Cypress Club, a New Urbanist development in Dean Park. (Then, courtesy Southwest Florida Historical Society.)

Midwesterner Clarence Bennett Chadwick, the inventor of forgery-proof checks, and his wife, Rosamond Lee Rouse Chadwick, a concert singer of national acclaim, purchased this splendid Mediterranean Revival–style house in 1925. The law firm of Garvin and Tripp now occupies this house, which was constructed to weather South Florida's hurricanes. The house's walls were one foot thick. It is sensibly perched on a hill across from the river on First Street. (Then, courtesy Southwest Florida Historical Society.)

Brothers Mike, Rocco, and Joseph W. Pavese built the St. Charles Hotel in 1925. Originally known as the Seminole Hotel, it had the distinction of two identical entrances on Jackson and Lee Streets. Moderne adornments such as half-moon awnings echo the Jazz Age. A passageway on the second floor extended over the parking area and connected the guest areas. In the mid-1980s, the First Baptist Church built a new activities building on the site. (Then, courtesy Southwest Florida Historical Society.)

Vernon G. Widerquist and his bride, Johnette Odom, married and moved into their just-finished home on Rhode Island Avenue on January 1, 1921. One of the first houses to be built in Dean Park, the Widerquist-Thompson house exhibits many characteristics of a Craftsman bungalow, including a low-pitched roof, wide eaves, and a porch with pyramidal columns. One of the most desirable neighborhoods during the boom times of the 1920s, today this historic area is experiencing a renaissance. (Then, courtesy Southwest Florida Museum of History.)

BUSINESSES AND BUILDINGS

The interior of Stewart's Drug Store in the 1920s captures the era of the classic drugstore soda fountain. Standing at the counter is owner Willie Warner "W. W." Stewart with Lillian Franklin "Bob" Stewart at the register and Peewee Franklin behind the counter. The business was located on the south side of Main Street between Jackson and Hendry Streets. (Then, courtesy Thomas Goolsby Stewart, Ph.D., and Carolyn Webber.)

Ben King's garage and filling station was Fort Myers's first business to cater exclusively to the dawning automobile age. The garage was located on the east side of Jackson Street just south of First Street. Note the vintage gas pump on the far right. Pictured from left to right are Littleton Yent, Clyde Langford, Ben King, Walter Thomas, Hal Frierson, Hunter Bryant, and Durwood Lynn. The Embarq building now stands on the site. (Then, courtesy Southwest Florida Historical Society.)

In 1905, Nathaniel H. Hunter (second from right) opened this pharmacy in the Bradford Building at First and Hendry Streets. For four decades, Hunter's Drug Store was a family concern. Hunter's brother, Dr. A. P. Hunter, and later their nephew, pharmacist Charles Hunter Brown, worked there. On the right (below) is Lee County's first sheriff, Thomas W. Langford. Today the storefront is part of the Florida Gulf Bank. (Then, courtesy Southwest Florida Historical Society.)

The general store that Robert Abner "R. A." Henderson Sr. opened in 1887 became one of the most successful in the region. The store ended its long history at this last of several locations, the southwest corner of Hendry Street and Anderson Avenue, which is now the home of Margie's Antiques on Martin Luther King Jr. Boulevard. In the 1929 photograph, R. A. Henderson Jr. and Sr. are seated in front of the business that once sold "everything for man or beast." (Then, courtesy Southwest Florida Historical Society.)

Guy B. Reynolds opened his two-story brick grocery store in 1905 near the northeast corner of Hendry and Oak (now Main) Streets. Oak Street was extended east to Jackson Street in the early 1920s. Reynolds and Sons catered to wealthy newcomers and tourists. In the early 1940s, the Edison Theatre opened on the corner, and a sturdy cow town general store ceded to art deco geometric accents and the escapism of wartime Hollywood. The theater is now an office building. (Then, courtesy Southwest Florida Historical Society.)

Harvie Earnhardt Heitman built the city's first brick building in 1898 on the northwest corner of First and Jackson Streets to replace his successful, frame-construction general store. In the 1920s, the Rembrandt Photography Studio was located on the second-floor corner. Heitman wielded significant influence in the business, civic, and political affairs of early Fort Myers. The high-rise skyline of West First Street illustrates how much things have changed since his time. (Then, courtesy State Archives of Florida.)

BUSINESSES AND BUILDINGS

In 1926, Chris's Lunch was a popular spot located on the southeast corner of Hendry and Bay Streets behind the Bradford Hotel. Christopher Demas and his wife, Bertha, managed the business, which was officially called C. D. Dairy Lunch. David Bull Jr. of Alva, who used to deliver eggs to the business with his father, suspects that he might be the young man in the photograph. Today the popular café is a parking lot for a law firm. (Then, courtesy Southwest Florida Historical Society.)

Owner Orris "O. M." Davison, mayor of Fort Myers from 1923 to 1926, and his friend Issac Perle "I. P." McSpadden started the Groceteria in 1920. Joining the new trend in self-service grocery shopping, they advertised, "We help those who help themselves." The store occupied the ground floor of a building on the southwest corner of Hendry and Main Streets, and apartment dwellers lived upstairs. A city-owned, mahogany-shaded parking lot now lies where customers discovered the novelty of self-service grocery shopping. (Then, courtesy Southwest Florida Historical Society.)

James A. Hendry built the future Lee County Bank in 1911 at Hendry and Main Streets. The hard-pine structure received a new stucco facade in 1927 and opened as the Lee County Bank, Title, and Trust Company. It reopened in 1934 as the Lee County Bank during the Great Depression. In the c. 1950 photograph, the bank sports a flamboyant sign of Gen. Robert E. Lee on his horse Traveler where Main Street Antiques and Collectibles does business today. (Then, courtesy Southwest Florida Museum of History.)

The Snack House in the Collier Arcade on Broadway ranks as one of the most popular eateries in Fort Myers's history. The town's social, political, and business life thrived there for 44 years. Jesse Winford "Win" Ellis opened the business in 1949 when Barron G. Collier needed a restaurant to serve his arcade's bus terminal. It was the first restaurant in town to be air-conditioned. A bank, a hair salon, and a restaurant currently occupy the old Snack House space. (Then, courtesy Southwest Florida Museum of History.)

During the gas-rationing days of World War II, Fort Myers residents could buy gas for about 25¢ per gallon or rent a bicycle at Vern Jungferman's Royal Palm Service Station on the southeast corner of Main Street and Broadway. He operated the station until 1946. The brick streets, globe-top gas pump, and two-pane car windshields in the vintage photograph evoke the era. Today the corner continues its automobile-centered use as a city-owned parking lot. (Then, courtesy Dickie Jungferman and Southwest Florida Historical Society.)

In 1946, Trent Bowen transformed a fountain with live alligators into a fresh-squeezed juice stand named the Patio Pauseway. Bowen also had the first soft-serve ice cream in town. The stand was situated in Patio de Leon, which connects Main, First, and Hendry Streets behind the Leon Building. To the right of the stand is the now-demolished theater, built in 1913 and sequentially named the Court, the Omar, the Ritz, and the Little Theatre. The fountain has been restored. (Then, courtesy Pete Bowen and Southwest Florida Historical Society.)

BUSINESSES AND BUILDINGS

CHAPTER 4

COMMUNITY SPACES, PUBLIC PLACES

The Jones-Walker Hospital on High Street was the first hospital in Fort Myers for African Americans. Opened in the late 1920s in the heart of the Dunbar community, it was named for Melissa Jones and Candis Walker who, along with Ivy Posey and Julia Barker, raised matching funds to build it. Dr. Edward Estevez Velasco was one of the first African American medical doctors to work in the community. This facility closed in 1947. (Then, courtesy Southwest Florida Historical Society.)

The Gwynne Institute, shown above in the 1920s, opened in October 1911 on the same site where Fort Myers's first public school had stood. It was named for Col. Andrew D. Gwynne, a winter visitor from Tennessee who wished to improve the town's educational facilities. Upon his death, Gwynne's family contributed $8,000, which was matched by citizens. A bond issue and additional school board funds made the school possible. The proud building served in an educational capacity until 2006. (Then, courtesy State Archives of Florida.)

COMMUNITY SPACES, PUBLIC PLACES

Although the engraving reads "Lee County High School," the 1924 yellow-brick structure (below) at Thompson and Fowler Streets was called Fort Myers High School. Built at a cost of $224,500, it was one of many public schools constructed during that decade of record population increases and demand for schools. The class of 1950 was the last to graduate in this building before a new high school opened. The Lee County Constitutional Complex now occupies the site. (Then, courtesy Southwest Florida Museum of History.)

The Methodist church in Fort Myers officially organized in 1879 with a congregation of more than 70 people. In 1903, the O'Neill Memorial Methodist Church, shown in the *c.* 1915 photograph (below) on First Street at Royal Palm Avenue, replaced an existing church on the same site. Hugh O'Neill, who built the Royal Palm Hotel across the street, donated the money for a new church in memory of his only son, Hugh O'Neill Jr. The existing First United Methodist Church opened in 1953. (Then, courtesy State Archives of Florida.)

Howell A. Parker built Phoenix Hall in 1890. Located in the heart of Fort Myers above Edward Lewis "E. L." Evans's general store on the southeast corner of First and Hendry Streets, it hosted community, arts, cultural, recreational, and political events for more than 20 years. In August 1914, the neoclassic-style First National Bank was erected on that corner. Today the city's first granite structure houses the law offices of Avery, Whigham, and Winesett. (Then, courtesy Southwest Florida Historical Society.)

The shady oasis of the Lee County Courthouse on Main Street is a reminder of Fort Myers's origins as a small, sleepy Southern town. The tranquility, however, belies the dramatic history of the courthouse. In October 1914, commissioner William H. Towles ordered the demolition of the existing courthouse so this modern neoclassical revival–style one would have to be built. In March 1989, it was listed in the National Register of Historic Places and subsequently underwent a $5 million restoration. (Then, courtesy Southwest Florida Historical Society.)

COMMUNITY SPACES, PUBLIC PLACES

Lee Memorial Hospital, which opened in October 1916 at Victoria and Grand Avenues, was constructed with lumber from the county courthouse that commissioner William H. Towles ordered demolished. At first, it was a modest two-story building with only four rooms for patients, but two additions increased the patient capacity during the next 25 years. The hospital was razed in 1965 after two decades as the Victoria Apartments, and the site is currently the Family Health Centers of Southwest Florida, Inc. (Then, courtesy Southwest Florida Historical Society.)

The city acquired this wood-frame house from Edward L. Evans and Carrie Belle Hendry Evans in 1921 for use as the first permanent city hall. The city then filled in the river's edge to create Evans Park, a place where citizens could enjoy a concert at the bandstand or play shuffleboard or a card game at the Tourist Club. The house was torn down in 1954 to make way for the second city hall, which was ultimately replaced by a bank. (Then, courtesy Southwest Florida Historical Society.)

The group of congregants above assembles at the Friendship Baptist Church after a church service. Situated on Orange Street just east of Cranford Avenue, this was the first of three locations for the church. Organized in 1912, it was one of the first black churches in Fort Myers. In 1950, the church moved to its current location on Palm Avenue after 20 years of planning and struggle. Another church stands on the site today. (Then, courtesy Southwest Florida Historical Society.)

In July 1928, the death of a 15-year-old Eagle Scout from spinal meningitis elicited such an outpouring of affection and community spirit that residents built a memorial in his honor. Contractors donated the construction materials, and volunteers provided the labor for the Thomas Goolsby Boy Scout Memorial in Evans Park. Pictured are Goolsby's nieces, Frances Juanita Stewart Jacoby (left) and Sarah Emily Stewart, around 1930. The memorial that was built on Heitman Street between First and Main Streets was torn down in 1973. (Then, courtesy Southwest Florida Museum of History.)

One of the oldest congregations in the Dunbar community suffered the loss of its church at Hough Street and Anderson Avenue during the devastating hurricane of September 1926. The Mount Olive African Methodist Episcopal Church dates to at least 1895. Around 1929, the church rebuilt on nearby Orange Street and Palm Avenue, which is still its home today. This section of Anderson Avenue (now Martin Luther King Jr. Boulevard) is a six-lane highway in the east downtown business district. (Then, courtesy Southwest Florida Historical Society.)

In 1911, the new Edgewood School in East Fort Myers opened with approximately 50 pupils. The two-story, wood-frame school, seen below around 1916, stood between Edgewood and Seminole Avenues just east of Tarpon Street. A new brick school was built northeast of it in 1924, and the old wood-frame school burned down in the late 1920s. In the mid-1990s, a larger school replaced the 1924 one. (Then, courtesy Southwest Florida Historical Society.)

COMMUNITY SPACES, PUBLIC PLACES

The Paul Laurence Dunbar School on High Street is pictured shortly after its construction in 1927. It has served the historic black community of Dunbar as a high school, a junior high school, and currently as an adult and community education center. Funded with community donations, public funds, and support from the Julius Rosenwald Fund, it duplicates the architectural plan of the Edison Park Elementary School. It was listed on the National Register of Historic Places in 1992. (Then, courtesy State Archives of Florida.)

The former U.S. Post Office at the corner of First and Jackson Streets is one of Fort Myers's most spectacular structures. Built by the Work Projects Administration, this neoclassical revival–style building opened in October 1933. Prior to its construction, Fort Myers's oldest house, the commanding officers headquarters built during the Seminole Indian Wars, was moved from the site. The post office has been reborn as the Sidney and Berne Davis Art Center, a cultural and architectural centerpiece of downtown. (Then, courtesy Southwest Florida Museum of History.)

The Fort Myers Public Library originated in March 1900 when the Fort Myers Woman's Club established a public reading room. After migrating to various locations during the next five decades, the library moved into its first permanent home in 1952 at this picturesque corner on Edwards Drive across from the Fort Myers Yacht Basin. It remained there until 1979. The renovated building is now the Greater Fort Myers Chamber of Commerce. (Then, courtesy Southwest Florida Museum of History.)

The 1958 photograph shows the Exhibition Hall on Edwards Drive only four years after its opening. The hall played an important role in Fort Myers's social and cultural life before its demolition in 2007. Elvis Presley, Pres. Gerald Ford, comedian Milton Berle, and other great names appeared there, and the memories of countless community events still echo in the minds of many Fort Myers citizens who loved the hall. (Then, courtesy Southwest Florida Museum of History.)

COMMUNITY SPACES, PUBLIC PLACES

CHAPTER 5

ON THE GO

The First and Hendry Street intersection is the historical heart of the business district. In the 1929 eastern view down First Street, the newly remodeled Bradford Hotel (left) is in its heyday. The hotel opened in 1905 and was named for the son of Tootie McGregor, who backed builder Harvie E. Heitman. Today the upper floors are the Bradford Apartments. (Then, courtesy Southwest Florida Museum of History.)

In 1905, everyday transportation involved ox- or horse-drawn wagons, as seen in the above photograph taken on Hendry Street in front of the Stone Block Building. Oxen not only provided transportation; they also powered sugar-cane mills, plowed fields, and hauled timber. Even in town, roads were often inadequate, rutted, and inconvenient; however, the arrival of the railroad in 1904 and, later, the automobile would change things. Now the renamed Leon Building features eateries, a cigar bar, and condominiums. (Then, courtesy Southwest Florida Historical Society.)

The Tootie McGregor Terry Fountain at Five Points was presented in 1913 to the city by Dr. Marshall O. Terry in memory of his wife, a benefactress, investor, and leading citizen. In the vintage photograph, Oak Street (left) and Anderson Avenue stretch into the distance, and a dog drinks from a lower trough of the marble and granite fountain. It was relocated to the Fort Myers Country Club in 1952. The Caloosahatchee Bridge overpass now dominates this location. (Then, courtesy Southwest Florida Historical Society.)

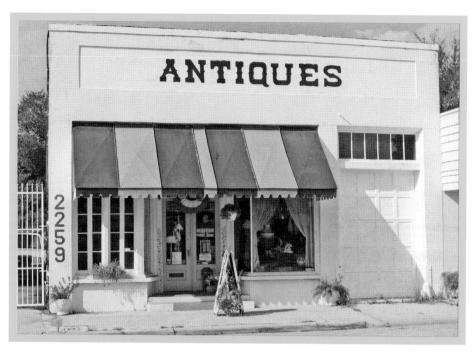

From 1923 until the 1960s, the Railway Express Agency on Peck Street handled cargo for the Atlantic Coastline Railroad, delivering in the early days by horse-and-wagon and later by trucks. Great quantities of produce and flowers were shipped, as well as the occasional live animal. Despite some exterior alterations since the 1925 photograph (below), the agency remains recognizable. Suitably, the Fancy Flamingo antiques and collectibles shop is located in this historic building today. (Then, courtesy Southwest Florida Museum of History.)

This Spanish-style railroad depot on Peck Street opened in 1924 to replace the old depot, which was constructed when the Atlantic Coastline Railroad arrived in Fort Myers in 1904. Shown above shortly after its opening, the depot played a significant role in the economic development and population growth of the city. In service until 1971, it stood vacant for a decade before being renovated and reopened in 1982 as the Fort Myers Historical Museum, later renamed the Southwest Florida Museum of History. (Then, courtesy Southwest Florida Museum of History.)

Bright new sidewalks welcome potential homeowners to the Poinciana Park subdivision in 1918. In the northward view (above) of McGregor Boulevard at Poinciana Avenue, the Caloosahatchee River is visible on the left, and Myron A. and Carrie Patch's house stands as a pioneer in the neighborhood. The boulevard was a trail for Native Americans, a military trail during the Second Seminole War, and a cattle trail as far back as the Civil War. (Then, courtesy Southwest Florida Historical Society.)

James E. Hendry Jr. sits in his automobile at the entrance to the new Edgewood subdivision in East Fort Myers about 1912. This entrance was at Superior Street and Palm Beach Boulevard, formerly called East First Street. As a horticulturist and member of the first city park board, Hendry is credited with making Fort Myers the "City of Palms" and was instrumental in bringing the Seaboard Railway to East Fort Myers in 1927. Commercial property has replaced the quaint gateway. (Then, courtesy State Archives of Florida.)

Tamiami Trail Tours' prime location at First and Jackson Streets attests to the growing importance of motor coaches as a form of transportation in 1925. Passengers on the company's first route enjoyed "natural" air-conditioning in open-air cars while traveling a dirt road between Fort Myers and Naples. Today the arches mark the spot where Barron G. Collier founded Collier West Coast Motor Lines in 1922, and the Franklin Arms stretches skyward in the background. (Then, courtesy Southwest Florida Museum of History.)

Pictured above, automobiles park by the entrance to the Edison estate on shell-rock McGregor Boulevard. Thomas and Mina Edison's long relationship with Fort Myers culminated with her gift of the entire estate to the city in 1947. In 1998, the City of Fort Myers bought neighboring Mangoes, the winter estate of Edison's friend Henry Ford. The Edison-Ford Winter Estates Foundation assumed operation of the estates in 2006, and both are on the National Register of Historic Places. (Then, courtesy Southwest Florida Museum of History.)

Citizens turned out for a procession when president-elect Herbert Hoover visited Fort Myers for Thomas Edison's 82nd birthday in February 1929 (above). The six-car procession is passing the Belmar Building on Broadway after a tour of the city. A two-story, Mediterranean-style building with a 50-foot frontage, the Belmar was completed in 1926 and today is the office of Goldstein, Buckley, Cechman, Rice, and Purtz. (Then, courtesy Southwest Florida Historical Society.)

Bayview Court is a walkway built in the mid-1920s to connect First and Bay Streets and to provide a throughway to the river's edge. In the early-1920s photograph, customers at the counter are visible through the window, as is the reflection of the photographer. Two attorneys occupy No. 11 Bayview today. This revitalizing of Bayview Court epitomizes a primary goal of downtown redevelopment: a pedestrian-friendly space where people can access shops, restaurants, and businesses while enjoying a river breeze. (Then, courtesy Southwest Florida Museum of History.)

In August 1926, two women cross First Street at the height of the boom, little knowing that September would bring a hurricane and the beginning of the Great Depression for South Florida. Today the south side of First Street, as seen from Dean Street, maintains the Mediterranean-style architectural features: parapets, tiled overhangs, ironwork balconies, and arched windows. Upstairs apartments and condominiums over storefronts echo the vibrancy of boom times. (Then, courtesy State Archives of Florida.)

In the early 1920s, a dynamic trio of developers— Henry Colquitt, George R. Sims, and Lucius Currian "L. C." Curtright—joined forces to buy properties and create Broadway between First and Main Streets. Broadway was paved and opened in early 1925. In the northward view of Broadway from Main Street, around 1930, the bell towers of the Colquitt Building (left foreground) and the Belmar punctuate the skyline. In the refurbishment of the Belmar Building, all its Mediterranean-style architectural features have been effaced. (Then, courtesy Southwest Florida Museum of History.)

Servicemen from Buckingham Airfield stand by the Morgan Dean Hotel around 1945. John Morgan Dean, a native of Rhode Island, opened the hotel in 1924 at the corner of First and Dean Streets. Built around the existing Sanchez boardinghouse, it featured a large dining room, brass-railed porches, and a rooftop solarium. The building retains its original name with the downstairs Morgan House, a restaurant and bar, and the upstairs Dean Apartments. (Then, courtesy Southwest Florida Historical Society.)

Franklin Hardware was a thriving business in 1950 at the corner of First Street and Broadway. Walter P. "W. P." Franklin founded the business in 1913 and opened this third location in 1937, where it remained in business for about 40 years. Since then, the building has undergone renovation, and features such as the art deco–style glass blocks, signage, and exterior tiles have reemerged, have been enhanced, or have been restored. (Then, courtesy State Archives of Florida.)

The McCrory's entrance on Hendry Street led to its popular lunch counter. The five-and-dime moved into the Earnhardt Building shortly after it was built in 1914 and stayed for more than 70 years. Other businesses on that stretch of Hendry Street around 1950 include the Royal Palm Studio, the Edison Theatre on the corner, and the Greystone Hotel across the street. (Then, courtesy Southwest Florida Museum of History.)

CHAPTER 6

JUST FOR FUN

In 1954, high school students collect coconuts for delivery to Pittsburgh Pirates fans at Forbes Field. Taking part in this whimsical promotion are, from left to right, Doris Swank Schneider, Pat Summey, Jo Ann White Horvath, Beth Prather Hyde, and Pat Batastini Scott. The Pirates completed their spring training in Fort Myers at Terry Park from 1955 to 1968. (Then, courtesy State Archives of Florida.)

Fourteen musicians organized the first Fort Myers band in November 1885, only months after the town formed. The band funded their sheet music and instrument purchases by selling subscriptions, and the town built a gazebo bandstand at the intersection of Second and Lee Streets. The band's first public appearance was serenading the honeymooning Thomas A. and Mina Edison at Seminole Lodge. New infrastructure and streetscaping are underway at the gazebo intersection. (Then, courtesy Southwest Florida Historical Society.)

Ambrose and Tootie McGregor donated 40 acres for the Fort Myers Yacht and County Club. This clubhouse, pictured below around 1911, was so well constructed by Manuel S. Gonzalez that it was used until it was demolished in 1980. The land became Terry Park, the perfect venue for Connie Mack to bring the Philadelphia Athletics to Fort Myers in 1924, initiating the city's tradition of hosting spring training for Major League Baseball teams. (Then, courtesy State Archives of Florida.)

The town's music scene got a boost when Francis W. Perry, a well-known composer, reorganized the Fort Myers Concert Band around 1900. By the World War I era, the Fort Myers band sported sharp professional uniforms. Around 1920, the band marches westward in front of the Lee County courthouse on Main Street, visible on the right. The band's venues throughout the years included the Pleasure Pier, holiday events, street dances, and park concerts. Today the landmark oak and banyan trees shade the band's route. (Then, courtesy Southwest Florida Historical Society.)

Built in 1915 by brothers Gilmer and Harvie Heitman, the Arcade Theatre has an entrance on First Street and this one on Bay Street, shown in the 1920s photograph. A 1991 benefit organized by the city and ballet star Mikhail Baryshnikov saved and restored this cultural treasure. Now the permanent home of the vibrant Florida Repertory Theatre, the vaudeville-era theater has returned to its roots with live performance. (Then, courtesy Southwest Florida Museum of History.)

The Edison Pageant of Light Grande Parade on First Street (above) expresses post–World War II exuberance and pride. The pageant's beginnings can be traced to the Conquista de Florida celebration, which started in 1917, but the Pageant of Light did not officially originate until 1938. Traditional festivities such as the parade and coronation continue, but events such as the City of Palms Block Party, Crafts on the River, the Regional Science and Inventors Fairs, and the Young Artists Awards have been added. (Then, courtesy Southwest Florida Historical Society.)

The *c.* 1945 parade (below) pays tribute to Fort Myers's cow town past, a time when cattle were herded down streets onto boats destined for the Cuban cattle market via Punta Rassa. Cowboys and cowgirls ride past the Colquitt Building (left) and the Collier/Post Office Arcade (right center) on Broadway. Built in 1925, this mixed-use, open-air structure remains one of the architectural delights of downtown. The post office, which was rented to the government for only $1 per year, created a high-traffic area and exemplified the New Urbanism guiding downtown redevelopment today. (Then, courtesy Southwest Florida Historical Society.)

In 1961, shuffleboard aficionados could play on the courts across from the Fort Myers Yacht Basin on Edwards Drive. The yacht basin and riverfront park, opened in 1939, were two of the Work Projects Administration's projects that helped transform Fort Myers into a thriving post–World War II city. The Hall of Fifty States, the only remnant of the 1927 Pleasure Pier, remains, but the adjacent shuffleboard courts were bulldozed in 2007. (Then, courtesy State Archives of Florida.)

TRANSITIONS AND
REINVENTION

The scene in front of Hunter's Drugstore conveys the joy that seized Fort Myers when "The War to End All Wars" ended on Armistice Day, November 11, 1918. The town celebrated with a parade and the closing of shops. Pictured from left to right are Esther Sherouse, ? Black, Sara Yelvington, Annabelle Hand, and Charles Bell Jennings. (Then, courtesy Southwest Florida Historical Society.)

Built in 1905 by Dr. Benjamin P. Matheson, the Stone Block Building housed the First National Bank and the second-floor Leon Hotel. The Mediterranean, Egyptian, and Moroccan motifs of today date to Peter Tonnelier's purchase of and remodeling of the building in 1912. Ironically, almost a century after the city installed the clay water and sewer pipes visible in the *c.* 1911 photograph, the city is replacing them. (Then, courtesy Southwest Florida Museum of History.)

TRANSITIONS AND REINVENTION

In 1907, Frank Graham of Brooklyn, New York, purchased land on the corner of Oak and Monroe Streets to build the 50-room Hotel Kenmore, a smart move in a town with a burgeoning tourist industry and a new railroad. A two-story expansion in 1917 included a rotunda so guests had open-air access to delicious South Florida air. Hotel Indigo, a seven-story, boutique-style hotel, will soon grace the site and carry on the tradition of welcoming visitors to Fort Myers. (Then, courtesy Southwest Florida Historical Society.)

The 1925 photograph (below) from the original sales brochure for the Edison Park subdivision shows the statue *Rachel at the Well*, also known as *The Spirit of Fort Myers*, by sculptor Helmut von Zengen. Developer James Newton, a friend of Thomas Edison, commissioned the statue, which stands across the street from the inventor's home. Mina Edison spoke to Newton on behalf of women who were offended by the maiden's nudity, and he agreed to drape Rachel with a toga. (Then, courtesy Southwest Florida Historical Society.)

TRANSITIONS AND REINVENTION

The Richards Professional Building (above, left) was known as the Pythian Building when Albertus A. "Bertie" Gardner built it on Hendry Street in 1924. The four-story, Italianate-style structure had the first elevator in town. In the 1925 photograph, the four-story Robb and Stucky Building stands beside it. In 1945, R. Q. Richards purchased the Pythian Building and changed its name. The Robb and Stucky furniture store moved in the late 1960s and evolved into a company with stores in four states. (Then, courtesy Southwest Florida Museum of History.)

The Mediterranean-style Elks Lodge on First Street is pictured above shortly after its construction in October 1925. When the Depression hit, the city assumed ownership of the property. Situated on the river just east of the Edison Bridge, it served as a tourists club, a USO during World War II, the short-lived Thomas Alva Edison College, the American Legion Post No. 38, and the public library. The Cypress Club, a high-rise, New Urbanist development, is destined for the site. (Then, courtesy Southwest Florida Historical Society.)

Henry Ford chose the design for the Mediterranean-style Sykes and Hill Garage. Completed in January 1926 for $60,000, it operated as a car dealership until 1963, after which it was renovated as an office building and renamed the Smith Building. It was briefly a county courthouse annex before being demolished in 1990. Now it is part of the ever-expanding Lee County Justice Center. (Then, courtesy Southwest Florida Historical Society.)

The Lee County Museum opened in the mid-1930s, the creation of Mrs. C. E. Briggs, a curator and collector, and Bertha M. Boomer, a visual artist, musician, instructor, and member of the Koreshan Unity Utopian Society community. The converted service station offered art classes, exhibits, programs, and discussions. This building at the nexus of Cleveland Avenue, Cortez Boulevard, and Edison Avenue became Gorley's Store in the 1940s. Students at nearby Edison Elementary School believed that the bell tower was haunted. (Then, courtesy Southwest Florida Historical Society.)

TRANSITIONS AND REINVENTION

A large bowling-pin sign marked the location of the Royal Palm Bowling Center on Monroe Street between First and Main Streets around 1945. Coolidge Sign Service is just to its north. In those days before automatic pin-setters, schoolboys could earn extra money for setting pins on the eight lanes. Now the imposing Federal Courthouse occupies the entire block along Monroe Street where once the rumble of bowling balls and the crash of pins could be heard. (Then, courtesy Southwest Florida Museum of History.)

In the 1936 photograph, the Gulf Refining filling station at First and Fowler Streets offers the shade of a poinciana tree, a cold drink, and a riverside bench. Constructed in 1930 only a block from the Edison Bridge, it was situated to capitalize on the tourist traffic streaming down the recently completed Tamiami Trail. The gabled roof of the Royal Palm Hotel provides a picturesque background. Today a vacant lot occupies the space. (Then, courtesy Southwest Florida Historical Society.)

TRANSITIONS AND REINVENTION

The Civic Center facing the river on Edwards Drive at Hendry Street welcomed countless soldiers stationed in Fort Myers at Buckingham and Page Fields during World War II. Constructed in 1943 with materials from the dismantled Pleasure Pier, it stood beside the Hall of Fifty States. As seen in the *c.* 1947 photograph, the building served as the Lee County Chamber of Commerce after the war. The center was demolished in 2007, leaving the neighboring hall alone on the site. (Then, courtesy Southwest Florida Historical Society.)

Pictured below is the Earnhardt Block on First Street around 1940. The Rendezvous restaurant and cocktail lounge occupies the corner of the 1910 Bank of Fort Myers Building. The Miller Building is adjacent to it, followed by the magnificent 193-foot-long Earnhardt Building, which was built in 1914 by Harvie Earnhardt Heitman. Today restaurants, shops, offices, and the Earnhardt Condominium bring energy to Fort Myers's most historic block between Jackson and Hendry Streets. (Then, courtesy Southwest Florida Museum of History.)

TRANSITIONS AND REINVENTION

A Publix supermarket at Clifford Street and McGregor Boulevard opened in 2007 on the spot where the Dairy Pleeze ice cream shop stood in the 1950s shortly before the development of the Boulevard Plaza. The famous royal palms that inspired the name "City of Palms" line the thoroughfare named in memory of Fort Myers benefactor Ambrose McGregor. Further residential and commercial development is planned for this 12-acre parcel named First Street Village. (Then, courtesy Southwest Florida Historical Society.)

In bustling downtown Fort Myers in the mid-1950s, the Belk-Lindsey Department Store and Wimberly's Drug Store anchored the heart of the business district at First and Hendry Streets. First Street stores included Sears, Roebuck, and Company; J. C. Penney; McCrory's; Bay Drugs; Flossie Hill's Ladies Department Store; Sidney Davis Men's Shop; and Kress. Today's eastern view is remarkably similar, although a bank has replaced the department store and high-rise residences loom on the skyline. (Then, courtesy State Archives of Florida.)

TRANSITIONS AND REINVENTION

Fort Myers's downtown redevelopment has altered few views as profoundly as this one. Initially, this field called League Park was a playground for children, a campground for the circus, and a practice field for the high school football team. In January 1960, Boulevard Plaza opened on McGregor Boulevard, inaugurating the age of the mall and drawing business activity from the downtown core. Today's skyline documents condominium history, from the 1963 Riverside Club (left), to the five towers of High Point Place. (Then, courtesy Southwest Florida Historical Society.

ACROSS AMERICA, PEOPLE ARE DISCOVERING SOMETHING WONDERFUL. *THEIR HERITAGE.*

Arcadia Publishing is the leading local history publisher in the United States. With more than 3,000 titles in print and hundreds of new titles released every year, Arcadia has extensive specialized experience chronicling the history of communities and celebrating America's hidden stories, bringing to life the people, places, and events from the past. To discover the history of other communities across the nation, please visit:

www.arcadiapublishing.com

Customized search tools allow you to find regional history books about the town where you grew up, the cities where your friends and family live, the town where your parents met, or even that retirement spot you've been dreaming about.